Great Works

Instructional Guides for Literature

Alexander and the Terrible, Horrible, No Good, Very Bad Day

A guide for the book by Judith Viorst
Great Works Author: Debra J. Housel

SHELL EDUCATION

Publishing Credits

Jill K. Mulhall, M.Ed., Editor

Image Credits

Howard McWilliam (cover, p. 11); Shutterstock (p. 14, p. 24, p. 25, p. 31, p. 32, p. 34, p. 36, p. 42, p. 47, p. 54); Timothy J. Bradley (p. 21)

Resource

Australian Geographic (pg. 54)
http://www.australiangeographic.com.au/blogs/ag-blog/2013/06/huge-feral-cats-wreaking-havoc-in-arnhem-land/

Standards

© 2007 Teachers of English to Speakers of Other Languages, Inc. (TESOL)
© 2007 Board of Regents of the University of Wisconsin System. World-Class Instructional Design and Assessment (WIDA)
© Copyright 2010. National Governors Association Center for Best Practices and Council of Chief State School Officers. All rights reserved.

Shell Education

5301 Oceanus Drive
Huntington Beach, CA 92649-1030
http://www.shelleducation.com
ISBN 978-1-4807-6910-6
© 2015 Shell Educational Publishing, Inc.

Table of Contents

How to Use This Literature Guide

Today's standards demand rigor and relevance in the reading of complex texts. The units in this series guide teachers in a rich and deep exploration of worthwhile works of literature for classroom study. The most rigorous instruction can also be interesting and engaging!

Many current strategies for effective literacy instruction have been incorporated into these instructional guides for literature. Throughout the units, text-dependent questions are used to determine comprehension of the book as well as student interpretation of the vocabulary words. The books chosen for the series are complex and are exemplars of carefully crafted works of literature. Close reading is used throughout the units to guide students toward revisiting the text and using textual evidence to respond to prompts orally and in writing. Students must analyze the story elements in multiple assignments for each section of the book. All of these strategies work together to rigorously guide students through their study of literature.

The next few pages describe how to use this guide for a purposeful and meaningful literature study. Each section of this guide is set up in the same way to make it easier for you to implement the instruction in your classroom.

Theme Thoughts

The great works of literature used throughout this series have important themes that have been relevant to people for many years. Many of the themes will be discussed during the various sections of this instructional guide. However, it would also benefit students to have independent time to think about the key themes of the book.

Before students begin reading, have them complete the *Pre-Reading Theme Thoughts* (page 13). This graphic organizer will allow students to think about the themes outside the context of the story. They'll have the opportunity to evaluate statements based on important themes and defend their opinions. Be sure to keep students' papers for comparison to the *Post-Reading Theme Thoughts* (page 58). This graphic organizer is similar to the pre-reading activity. However, this time, students will be answering the questions from the point of view of one of the characters in the book. They have to think about how the character would feel about each statement and defend their thoughts. To conclude the activity, have students compare what they thought about the themes before they read the book to what the characters discovered during the story.

Pre-Reading Picture Walks

For each section in this literature guide, there are suggestions for how to introduce the text to students. Teachers share information in a visual format and ask students to evaluate the content. Students must use the information presented in the illustrations to discuss what they are about to read and make predictions about the sections.

How to Use This Literature Guide (cont.)

Vocabulary

Each teacher reference vocabulary overview page has definitions and sentences about how key vocabulary words are used in the section. These words should be introduced and discussed with students. Students will use these words in different activities throughout the book.

On some of the vocabulary student pages, students are asked to answer text-related questions about vocabulary words from the sections. The following question stems will help you create your own vocabulary questions if you'd like to extend the discussion.

- How does this word describe _____'s character?
- How does this word connect to the problem in this story?
- How does this word help you understand the setting?
- Tell me how this word connects to the main idea of this story.
- What visual pictures does this word bring to your mind?
- Why do you think the author used this word?

At times, you may find that more work with the words will help students understand their meanings and importance. These quick vocabulary activities are a good way to further study the words.

- Students can play vocabulary concentration. Make one set of cards that has the words on them and another set with the definitions. Then, have students lay them out on the table and play concentration. The goal of the game is to match vocabulary words with their definitions. For early readers or English language learners, the two sets of cards could be the words and pictures of the words.
- Students can create word journal entries about the words. Students choose words they think are important and then describe why they think each word is important within the book. Early readers or English language learners could instead draw pictures about the words in a journal.
- Students can create puppets and use them to act out the vocabulary words from the stories. Students may also enjoy telling their own character-driven stories using vocabulary words from the original stories.

How to Use This Literature Guide *(cont.)*

Analyzing the Literature

After you have read each section with students, hold a small-group or whole-class discussion. Provided on the teacher reference page for each section are leveled questions. The questions are written at two levels of complexity to allow you to decide which questions best meet the needs of your students. The Level 1 questions are typically less abstract than the Level 2 questions. These questions are focused on the various story elements, such as character, setting, and plot. Be sure to add further questions as your students discuss what they've read. For each question, a few key points are provided for your reference as you discuss the book with students.

Reader Response

In today's classrooms, there are often great readers who are below average writers. So much time and energy is spent in classrooms getting students to read on grade level that little time is left to focus on writing skills. To help teachers include more writing in their daily literacy instruction, each section of this guide has a literature-based reader response prompt. Each of the three genres of writing is used in the reader responses within this guide: narrative, informative/explanatory, and opinion. Before students write, you may want to allow them time to draw pictures related to the topic.

Guided Close Reading

Within each section of this guide, it is suggested that you closely reread a portion of the text with your students. Page numbers are given, but since some versions of the books may have different page numbers, the sections to be reread are described by location as well. After rereading the section, there are a few text-dependent questions to be answered by students.

Working space has been provided to help students prepare for the group discussion. They should record their thoughts and ideas on the activity page and refer to it during your discussion. Rather than just taking notes, you may want to require students to write complete responses to the questions before discussing them with you.

Encourage students to read one question at a time and then go back to the text and discover the answer. Work with students to ensure that they use the text to determine their answers rather than making unsupported inferences. Suggested answers are provided in the answer key.

How to Use This Literature Guide *(cont.)*

Guided Close Reading *(cont.)*

The generic open-ended stems below can be used to write your own text-dependent questions if you would like to give students more practice.

- What words in the story support . . . ?
- What text helps you understand . . . ?
- Use the book to tell why _____ happens.
- Based on the events in the story, . . . ?
- Show me the part in the text that supports . . . .
- Use the text to tell why . . . .

Making Connections

The activities in this section help students make cross-curricular connections to mathematics, science, social studies, fine arts, or other curricular areas. These activities require higher-order thinking skills from students but also allow for creative thinking.

Language Learning

A special section has been set aside to connect the literature to language conventions. Through these activities, students will have opportunities to practice the conventions of standard English grammar, usage, capitalization, and punctuation.

Story Elements

It is important to spend time discussing what the common story elements are in literature. Understanding the characters, setting, plot, and theme can increase students' comprehension and appreciation of the story. If teachers begin discussing these elements in early childhood, students will more likely internalize the concepts and look for the elements in their independent reading. Another very important reason for focusing on the story elements is that students will be better writers if they think about how the stories they read are constructed.

In the story elements activities, students are asked to create work related to the characters, setting, or plot. Consider having students complete only one of these activities. If you give students a choice on this assignment, each student can decide to complete the activity that most appeals to him or her. Different intelligences are used so that the activities are diverse and interesting to all students.

How to Use This Literature Guide (cont.)

Culminating Activity

At the end of this instructional guide is a creative culminating activity that allows students the opportunity to share what they've learned from reading the book. This activity is open ended so that students can push themselves to create their own great works within your language arts classroom.

Comprehension Assessment

The questions in this section require students to think about the book they've read as well as the words that were used in the book. Some questions are tied to quotations from the book to engage students and require them to think about the text as they answer the questions.

Response to Literature

Finally, students are asked to respond to the literature by drawing pictures and writing about the characters and stories. A suggested rubric is provided for teacher reference.

Correlation to the Standards

Shell Education is committed to producing educational materials that are research and standards based. As part of this effort, we have correlated all of our products to the academic standards of all 50 states, the District of Columbia, the Department of Defense Dependents Schools, and all Canadian provinces.

Purpose and Intent of Standards

Standards are designed to focus instruction and guide adoption of curricula. Standards are statements that describe the criteria necessary for students to meet specific academic goals. They define the knowledge, skills, and content students should acquire at each level. Standards are also used to develop standardized tests to evaluate students' academic progress. Teachers are required to demonstrate how their lessons meet standards. Standards are used in the development of all of our products, so educators can be assured they meet high academic standards.

How to Find Standards Correlations

To print a customized correlation report of this product for your state, visit our website at http://www.shelleducation.com and follow the online directions. If you require assistance in printing correlation reports, please contact our Customer Service Department at 1-877-777-3450.

Correlation to the Standards (cont.)

Standards Correlation Chart

The lessons in this book were written to support the Common Core College and Career Readiness Anchor Standards. The following chart indicates which lessons address the anchor standards.

Common Core College and Career Readiness Anchor Standard	Section
CCSS.ELA-Literacy.CCRA.R.1—Read closely to determine what the text says explicitly and to make logical inferences from it; cite specific textual evidence when writing or speaking to support conclusions drawn from the text.	Analyzing the Literature Sections 1–4; Guided Close Reading Sections 1–4; Story Elements Sections 2, 4; Making Connections Sections 2–3
CCSS.ELA-Literacy.CCRA.R.2—Determine central ideas or themes of a text and analyze their development; summarize the key supporting details and ideas.	Analyzing the Literature Sections 1–4; Guided Close Reading Sections 1–4; Making Connections Section 4; Post-Reading Theme Thoughts
CCSS.ELA-Literacy.CCRA.R.3—Analyze how and why individuals, events, or ideas develop and interact over the course of a text.	Analyzing the Literature Sections 1–4; Guided Close Reading Sections 1–4; Story Elements Sections 1–4; Post-Reading Theme Thoughts
CCSS.ELA-Literacy.CCRA.R.4—Interpret words and phrases as they are used in a text, including determining technical, connotative, and figurative meanings, and analyze how specific word choices shape meaning or tone.	Vocabulary Activities Sections 1–4
CCSS.ELA-Literacy.CCRA.R.5—Analyze the structure of texts, including how specific sentences, paragraphs, and larger portions of the text (e.g., a section, chapter, scene, or stanza) relate to each other and the whole.	Making Connections Section 3; Post-Reading Response to Literature
CCSS.ELA-Literacy.CCRA.R.6—Assess how point of view or purpose shapes the content and style of a text.	Story Elements Section 3; Post-Reading Theme Thoughts
CCSS.ELA-Literacy.CCRA.R.7—Integrate and evaluate content presented in diverse media and formats, including visually and quantitatively, as well as in words.	Pre-Reading Picture Walk Sections 1–4
CCSS.ELA-Literacy.CCRA.R.10—Read and comprehend complex literary and informational texts independently and proficiently.	Entire Unit
CCSS.ELA-Literacy.CCRA.W.1—Write arguments to support claims in an analysis of substantive topics or texts using valid reasoning and relevant and sufficient evidence.	Story Elements Sections 2–3; Reader Response Sections 3–4

Common Core College and Career Readiness Anchor Standard	Section
CCSS.ELA-Literacy.CCRA.W.2—Write informative/explanatory texts to examine and convey complex ideas and information clearly and accurately through the effective selection, organization, and analysis of content.	Reader Response Section 1; Making Connections Section 2
CCSS.ELA-Literacy.CCRA.W.3—Write narratives to develop real or imagined experiences or events using effective technique, well-chosen details and well-structured event sequences.	Reader Response Section 2
CCSS.ELA-Literacy.CCRA.W.4—Produce clear and coherent writing in which the development, organization, and style are appropriate to task, purpose, and audience.	Reader Response Sections 1–4; Language Learning Section 1; Story Elements Sections 2–3
CCSS.ELA-Literacy.CCRA.L.1—Demonstrate command of the conventions of standard English grammar and usage when writing or speaking.	Language Learning Sections 1, 3–4
CCSS.ELA-Literacy.CCRA.L.2—Demonstrate command of the conventions of standard English capitalization, punctuation, and spelling when writing.	Reader Response Sections 1–4; Language Learning Section 2–3; Post-Reading Response to Literature
CCSS.ELA-Literacy.CCRA.L.6—Acquire and use accurately a range of general academic and domain-specific words and phrases sufficient for reading, writing, speaking, and listening at the college and career readiness level; demonstrate independence in gathering vocabulary knowledge when encountering an unknown term important to comprehension or expression.	Vocabulary Activities Sections 1–4

TESOL and WIDA Standards

The lessons in this book promote English language development for English language learners. The following TESOL and WIDA English Language Development Standards are addressed through the activities in this book:

- **Standard 1:** English language learners communicate for social and instructional purposes within the school setting.

- **Standard 2:** English language learners communicate information, ideas and concepts necessary for academic success in the content area of language arts.

About the Author—Judith Viorst

Judith Stahl was born in New Jersey in 1931. She attended Rutgers University and earned a bachelor's degree in history. In 1960, she married Milton Viorst, who is a political writer. The couple resides in Washington, D.C. Viorst earned another degree from the Washington Psychoanalytic Institute where she worked as a research affiliate.

Her most famous children's book is *Alexander and the Terrible, Horrible, No Good, Very Bad Day*, which has sold over two million copies. In addition, Viorst is the author of many fiction and nonfiction books for adults and children. As a newspaper columnist, she has written for *The New York Times* and *The Washington Post*. She served as a contributing editor for *REDBOOK* magazine.

The National Research Center for Women & Families awarded Viorst the 2011 Foremother Award for Lifetime Achievement. This award is given annually to three women who have spent their lives improving the lives of adults and children.

Possible Texts for Text Comparisons

There are three more books about Alexander, including *Alexander, Who Used to Be Rich Last Sunday*; *Alexander, Who's Not (Do You Hear Me? I Mean It!) Going to Move*; and *Alexander, Who's Trying His Best to Be the Best Boy Ever*.

Cross-Curricular Connection

This book can be used in a health unit about expressing emotions or managing family life. It could also be tied to a geography unit about Australia.

Book Summary of *Alexander and the Terrible, Horrible, No Good, Very Bad Day*

From the moment that Alexander wakes up, he knows he is going to have an awful day. He has gum in his hair and drops his sweater under running water. His two brothers find prizes in their cereal boxes, and he does not. When he complains that he is too cramped in the back seat of the car, no one acknowledges him. At school things only get worse. His teacher does not like his drawing of an invisible castle, and he forgets to say "16" when he is counting. His friend Paul names two other boys as his "best friends." To top it off, Alexander's mother forgets to include a dessert with his lunch.

Later, the dentist gives Alexander's brothers clean bills of health and Alexander an appointment to come back to get a cavity filled. He falls in the mud and his brothers tease him, but his mother only sees Alexander punch Nick. At the shoe store, his brothers get awesome new sneakers. The store is out of the type of sneakers Alexander wants.

When they go to pick up his dad at the office, Alexander manages to knock books off the desk and create havoc with the photocopier. At dinner his mother serves lima beans, which he hates. During his bath, the water is the wrong temperature, he gets soap in his eyes, and he loses a marble down the drain. He ends the day in bed in his most hated pair of pajamas with a burned-out night light. It has been a terrible, horrible, no good, very bad day. Alexander's mom says some days are like that.

There is a musical stage version of the story, which features the same characters and plot (with additional misadventures). Different theater companies offer it around the nation, but it is not available on DVD. Walt Disney Pictures also filmed a movie adaptation of the book in 2014. However, the movie contains many differences from the book.

Instructional Guide Sections

There are four sections in this guide. The book is divided as listed below:

- Section 1 covers the Morning, which is pages 1–5.
- Section 2 covers At School, which is pages 6–11.
- Section 3 covers After School, which is pages 12–21.
- Section 4 covers the Evening, which is pages 22–28.

Possible Texts for Text Sets

- Allard, Harry. *Miss Nelson Is Missing!* HMH Books for Young Readers, 1985.
- Mosel, Arlene. *Tikki Tikki Tembo*. Square Fish Publishing, 2007.
- Stanek, Robert. *The Bugville Critters Have a Bad Day*. Reagent Press Books for Young Readers, 2009.
- Viorst, Judith. *I'll Fix Anthony*. Atheneum Books for Young Readers, 1988.

Pre-Reading Theme Thoughts

Directions: Read each statement below. Draw a picture of a happy face or a sad face in the column next to it. The face should show how you feel about the statement. Then, use words to say what you think about each statement.

Statement	How Do You Feel? 😊 ☹️	Explain Your Answer
You find a prize in a cereal box.		
Sometimes you have to share your friend with other friends.		
You have a cavity.		
A parent blames you when it isn't your fault.		

Pre-Reading Picture Walk

1. Show students the front cover of the book. Ask them to identify the title, the author, and the illustrator for the story.

2. Explain that good readers make predictions before reading. A prediction is making a guess about characters or what will happen in a story. One way to do this is to examine the pictures before reading.

3. Ask students to identify the main character on the cover. (*Alexander, who is named in the title of the book.*) Based on the front cover illustration, ask "How old is Alexander?" (*He appears to be between 5 and 8 years old.*)

4. Turn to the first page with a picture. Cover the text. Have students make predictions about Alexander's mood based on his facial expression.

5. Turn to the next page and cover the text. Have students make a prediction about the identities of the three boys sitting at the table. (*They are three brothers.*)

6. Cover the text on the next page. Have students look at Alexander's face and predict if his mood is improving, getting worse, or staying the same.

Vocabulary Overview

Key words and phrases from this section are provided below with definitions and sentences about how the words are used in the story. Introduce and discuss these important vocabulary words with students. If you think these words or other words in the story warrant more time devoted to them, there are suggestions in the introduction for other vocabulary activities (page 5).

word	Definition	Sentence about Text
sweater	a warm, knitted top	Alexander's **sweater** gets wet, so he can't wear it.
terrible	awful; upsetting	When he wakes up, Alexander thinks he will have a **terrible** day.
horrible	very bad; unpleasant	Alexander's day gets more **horrible** by the minute.
Undercover Agent	a spy; a person who works in a secret way to catch criminals or collect information	Nick finds a Junior **Undercover Agent** ring in his cereal.
code	a set of letters, numbers, or symbols used to secretly send messages to someone	Nick can use his **code** ring to figure out secret messages.
Australia	the only country that is also a continent; it lies in the Southern Hemisphere below the equator	Alexander thinks moving to **Australia** sounds like a good idea.
car pool	a group of people who ride together each day to school or work	Mrs. Gibson drives students in the **car pool**.
scrunched	squeezed together too tightly	Alexander is **scrunched** in the back seat of the car.
smushed	smashed or crushed into something	Alexander complains that he is being **smushed**, but no one listens.
carsick	feeling nauseated while riding in a car	Alexander says he will be **carsick** if he doesn't get a different seat in the car.

Name _____ Date _____

Vocabulary Activity

Directions: Draw lines to complete the sentences.

Sentence Beginnings	Sentence Endings
Nick looks in his cereal box	**smushed** in the back seat.
Alexander drops his **sweater** in the sink	to school in a **car pool.**
Mrs. Gibson drives four children	as soon as Alexander wakes up.
Alexander says he is	and finds a Junior **Undercover Agent code** ring.
The **terrible** day begins	while the water is running.

Directions: Answer this question.

1. What does Alexander say would keep him from being **carsick**?

_____

_____

Analyzing the Literature

Provided below are discussion questions you can use in small groups, with the whole class, or for written assignments. Each question is written at two levels so you can choose the right question for each group of students. For each question, a few key points are provided for your reference as you discuss the book with students.

Story Element	Level 1	Level 2	Key Discussion Points
Setting	What is the setting of this story?	Where and at what time of day does the story begin?	The story takes place in Alexander's home (his bedroom and the kitchen) and later in Mrs. Gibson's car. It begins in the morning, when Alexander wakes up, gets dressed, eats breakfast, and leaves for school.
Plot	What is the problem?	Why does Alexander feel like no one cares about his problem?	Alexander is having a very bad day. To make matters worse, his brothers and Mrs. Gibson seem oblivious to his problem. His brothers are only concerned with their new toys. Mrs. Gibson doesn't acknowledge Alexander when he complains in the car.
Plot	What happens to Alexander in the bathroom?	What three events first make Alexander think he'll have a terrible day?	Alexander awakens with gum in his hair, trips over a skateboard, and drops his sweater into the sink while the water is running.
Character	Who are Nick and Anthony?	What do you think is Nick's and Anthony's relationship to Alexander?	Nick and Anthony are at the table eating cereal with Alexander. It is reasonable to predict that the three boys are siblings. Alexander appears to be the youngest of the boys.

Name _____ Date _____

Reader Response

Think

Alexander is having a terrible, horrible, no good, very bad day. To make matters worse, no one seems to notice. Think about a time when you had a bad day. Did anyone do something to help you feel better?

Informative/Explanatory Writing Prompt

Can you tell when someone else is having a bad day? How do you know? Describe what you can do to help someone who is having a bad day.

_____

_____

_____

_____

_____

_____

_____

_____

Guided Close Reading

Closely reread the first page of text in the book.

Directions: Think about these questions. In the space below, write ideas or draw pictures as you think. Be ready to share your answers.

❶ Use the text to describe the three bad things that happen to Alexander before breakfast.

❷ Which statement on the first page will be repeated on other pages of the book?

❸ The whole first page is written as a single sentence. Why did the author write it this way?

Name _____ Date _____

Making Connections-Visualize

Directions: Imagine that you open a box of cereal and get a Junior Undercover Agent code ring just like the one Nick gets. What does it look like? How is it used? Draw the Junior Undercover Agent code ring. Label its parts. Write a sentence to tell how it is used.

_____

_____

_____

Making Connections-Australian Vegemite

If he moves to Australia, Alexander could eat toast with Vegemite for breakfast. Vegemite is made of vegetables and yeast. It is a brown paste that tastes salty. Vegemite is used as a spread on toast, crackers, and sandwiches.

Directions: What do you put on toast? Color the slice of toast below to show its color and the color of what you put on it. Write a sentence telling about your slice of toast.

_____

_____

Name _____ Date _____

Language Learning–Writing a Friendly Letter

Directions: Imagine you are Alexander. Write a letter to a relative that describes your thoughts and feelings about all that happens before you even get to school.

Language Hints!

- Use a comma after your greeting.

- Use a comma after your closing.

_____

_____

_____

_____

_____

_____

_____

_____

_____

_____

Story Elements-Plot

Directions: Alexander has five bad things happen to him before he gets to school. Write a list of these events in the strips below. Cut out each event. Then, give the events to a friend to put in order of how they happened in the book. Check your friend's work.

Name _____ Date _____

Story Elements-Setting

Directions: Alexander says he wants to move to Australia. Australia is the only nation that is also a continent. Label six of the continents on the map below.

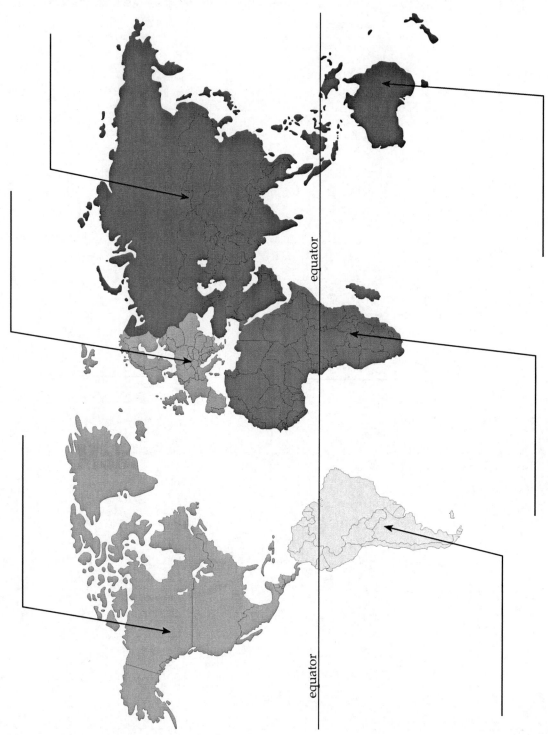

Pre-Reading Picture Walk

1. Remind students that good readers make predictions before reading. A prediction is making a guess about characters or what will happen in a story. One way to do this is to examine the pictures before reading.

2. Turn to the first page showing the children in school. Cover the text. Have students identify where Alexander is. Ask, "What activity are the students doing?" *(They are drawing pictures.)*

3. Move to the next page. Cover the text. Have students look at Alexander's face and predict if his mood is improving, getting worse, or staying the same.

4. Open to the next spread. Ask students to identify the setting. *(The children are on the playground.)* Have students make a prediction about who the three boys who have their arms around each other are. Ask, "Where is Alexander standing? What is he doing?" *(He is standing alone and yelling.)*

5. Turn to the page spread showing lunch. Cover the text. Tell students there is one sentence on the second page of this spread and have them guess what it is based on the look on Alexander's face. Then reveal the sentence and have the class read it aloud. *("It was a terrible, horrible, no good, very bad day.")*

Vocabulary Overview

Key words and phrases from this section are provided below with definitions and sentences about how the words are used in the story. Introduce and discuss these important vocabulary words with students. If you think these words or other words in the story warrant more time devoted to them, there are suggestions in the introduction for other vocabulary activities (page 5).

Word	Definition	Sentence about Text
invisible	impossible to see	Alexander's **invisible** drawing looks like a blank piece of paper.
castle	a large building with high, thick walls and towers that was built to protect against an attack	The teacher prefers another drawing over Alexander's **castle.**
tack	a short nail that has a sharp point and a flat head	It would hurt to sit on a sharp **tack.**
double-decker	something that has two layers or levels	Alexander hopes Paul's **double-decker** ice cream falls off its cone.
Hershey	an American company that makes and sells chocolate candy	Alexander is jealous that Albert gets a **Hershey** chocolate bar with lunch.
almonds	sweet, oval-shaped nuts	Some people like to add **almonds** to their chocolate for an extra sweet treat.
jelly roll	a thin sheet of cake spread with jelly that is then rolled into a cylinder shape	Paul's mother packed a **jelly roll** in his lunch.
coconut	the shredded white flesh inside of a large brown fruit that grows on a palm tree	Putting **coconut** on top adds a little flavor to a dessert.
sprinkles	tiny candies that are put on top of a sweet food	Ice cream cones may have **sprinkles** on top of them.
dessert	a sweet food eaten at the end of a meal	Alexander's mother forgets to pack him a **dessert.**

Vocabulary Activity

Directions: Complete each sentence below. Use one of the words listed.

Words from the Story

castle	coconut	double-decker	invisible	dessert

1. Alexander draws a(n) _____ picture.

2. Paul's jelly roll has _____ sprinkles on it.

3. The _____ picture should have shown a strong building.

4. Alexander's mom did not pack a _____ in his lunch.

5. Paul likes to eat _____ strawberry ice cream cones.

Directions: Answer this question.

6. What does Paul say to Alexander to upset him?

   _____

   _____

   _____

   _____

Analyzing the Literature

Provided below are discussion questions you can use in small groups, with the whole class, or for written assignments. Each question is written at two levels so you can choose the right question for each group of students. For each question, a few key points are provided for your reference as you discuss the book with students.

Story Element	Level 1	Level 2	Key Discussion Points
Setting	During school, where is Alexander?	In what three places do we see Alexander at school?	We see Alexander in the classroom, then on the playground, and finally in the lunchroom.
Character	Who does Alexander believe is his best friend?	What does Alexander discover about his best friend?	Alexander thinks that Paul is his best friend. He is shocked and upset when Paul announces that Alexander is only his third best friend after Philip and Albert.
Plot	What does Alexander say to Paul?	How do we know that Alexander loses his temper with Paul?	Alexander is clearly angry when he tells Paul he hopes he sits on a tack and that the next time he gets a strawberry double-decker ice cream cone it falls apart.
Character	Who is Mrs. Dickens?	What negative feedback does Alexander's teacher give him?	Mrs. Dickens is Alexander's teacher. She criticizes him three times before lunch: first for doing an invisible drawing of a castle, next for singing too loudly, and then for forgetting 16 when he is counting aloud.

Reader Response

Think

Paul hurts Alexander's feelings on the playground. Has a friend ever hurt your feelings?

Narrative Writing Prompt

Write about a time when a friend hurt your feelings.

_____

_____

_____

_____

_____

_____

_____

_____

_____

_____

Name _____ Date _____

Guided Close Reading

Closely reread the page where Alexander talks to Paul.

Directions: Think about these questions. In the space below, write ideas or draw pictures as you think. Be ready to share your answers.

❶ Use the text to describe how Alexander feels about what Paul says to him.

❷ Based on the events of the story, why does Alexander say mean things to Paul?

❸ What do you think Paul says to Alexander in response?

Making Connections—Healthy Foods

Directions: At lunch, Alexander finds out that his mother forgot to pack a dessert. Desserts are not as good for your body as other foods. Look at the illustration of the boys having lunch. Answer the questions.

1. What desserts are shown?

_____

_____

_____

2. What healthy foods are shown?

_____

_____

_____

3. What are some other healthy foods that parents pack in lunches?

_____

_____

_____

Making Connections-Australian Seasons

Directions: Alexander might be surprised by the seasons in Australia. They are the opposite of ours! We live above the equator. Australia is below the equator. So, it has winter when we have summer. Answer each question.

1. When it's  here, what season is it in Australia?

   _____

2. When it's  here, what season is it in Australia?

   _____

3. When it's  here, what season is it in Australia?

   _____

4. When it's  here, what season is it in Australia?

   _____

Language Learning–Question Marks

Directions: In the first column, write three questions you have for Alexander. In the second column, write his answers. Remember to follow the rules about question marks and capital letters.

Language Hints!

- Use a question mark at the end of a question.

- Start sentences with capital letters.

Questions for Alexander	Alexander's Answers

Directions: Answer this question.

1. Alexander asks two questions in this section. Who is he talking to? Why does the author choose to have him ask these questions?

_____

_____

_____

Name _____ Date _____

Story Elements–Character

Directions: In this section, we meet Alexander's friend Paul. On the lines below, write what you know about Paul and what you think about Paul.

Directions: Answer this question.

1. Do you think Paul is being mean or just honest?

_____

Story Elements–Plot

Directions: How did Alexander add to his terrible, horrible, no good, very bad day with his invisible castle drawing? Write an email to Alexander explaining how he made things worse.

From: | |

To: | Alexander |

Subject: | Invisible Castle Drawing |

| |

Pre-Reading Picture Walk

1. Remind students that good readers make predictions before reading. A prediction is making a guess about characters or what will happen in a story. One way to do this is to examine the pictures before reading.

2. Turn to the page spread at the dentist. Cover the text. Have students identify where Alexander is. Ask "Who else is there with Alexander?" *(Alexander is in a dentist's office with his mother, his two brothers, and the dentist.)*

3. Move to the next spread. Cover the text. Have students look at the pictures. Have students predict what happened to Alexander on the first page and what happened to him on the second page. *(First, Alexander hurt his foot. Then, he fell down or was knocked down by his brothers.)*

4. Open to the next page, covering the text. Ask students to identify the setting. *(They are on the sidewalk by the car.)* Have students make a prediction about how the mother is feeling. Ask, "What is the mother probably saying? Who is she talking to?" *(The mother looks angry and she is probably reprimanding her sons, who are fighting.)*

Vocabulary Overview

Key words and phrases from this section are provided below with definitions and sentences about how the words are used in the story. Introduce and discuss these important vocabulary words with students. If you think these words or other words in the story warrant more time devoted to them, there are suggestions in the introduction for other vocabulary activities (page 5).

Word	Definition	Sentence about Text
dentist	a doctor who takes care of people's teeth	The three brothers have their teeth checked by the dentist.
cavity	a hole in a tooth caused by decay	Alexander will have to have his cavity filled by the dentist.
elevator	a machine that carries people and things up or down to all the different levels in a building	The heavy elevator doors close on Alexander's foot.
crybaby	a teasing name for a person who cries too easily or complains all the time	Nick calls Alexander a crybaby after he falls in the mud.
scolded	angrily told someone they have done something wrong	Alexander's mother scolds him for hitting Nick.
sold out	having no more left	Alexander can't get the shoes he wants because his size is all sold out.
copying	making a duplicate (exact image) of something	The copying machine breaks when Alexander plays with it.
elbow	the joint where one's arm bends	The books on the father's desk get knocked off by Alexander's elbow.

Name _____ Date _____

Vocabulary Activity

Directions: Practice your vocabulary and writing skills. Write at least four sentences using words from the story. Make sure your sentences show what the words mean.

Words from the Story

dentist	elbow	cavity	elevator
crybaby	sold out	copying	scolded

_____

_____

_____

_____

_____

_____

_____

Directions: Answer this question.

1. What does the **copying** machine do after Alexander plays with it?

_____

Analyzing the Literature

Provided below are discussion questions you can use in small groups, with the whole class, or for written assignments. Each question is written at two levels so you can choose the right question for each group of students. For each question, a few key points are provided for your reference as you discuss the book with students.

Story Element	Level 1	Level 2	Key Discussion Points
Plot	What happens to Alexander in the dentist's office?	Why does Alexander look upset in the dentist's office? What makes it worse?	The dentist finds a cavity in one of Alexander's teeth. Alexander will have to come back and have it fixed. To make it worse, neither of Alexander's brothers have cavities.
Character	How does Nick behave after Alexander falls down?	What do we learn about Nick from the way he acts after Alexander falls down?	Nick mocks Alexander after he falls, calling him a crybaby. This tells us that, at least sometimes, Nick is not a very nice brother.
Character	What upsets Alexander in the shoe store?	Why didn't Alexander get the sneakers he wanted?	The shoe man tells Alexander that they're sold out of his first choice for shoes. Alexander's mother makes him buy plain white sneakers instead. Alexander is upset because his brothers get the colorful shoes they want.
Setting	Where does Alexander's father work?	What does the illustration of the office tell us about Alexander's father's job?	Alexander's father works in an office, doing some kind of a desk job. The illustration shows a desk, pencils and ink, books, a telephone, and a copying machine. Alexander's father wears a coat and tie.

Name _____ Date _____

Reader Response

Think

Alexander takes a tumble in a mud puddle. Think of a time you had a minor fall. What happened? Did you feel like crying?

Opinion Writing Prompt

Do you think Alexander was acting like a crybaby? Explain why or why not.

_____

_____

_____

_____

_____

_____

_____

_____

_____

Guided Close Reading

Closely reread the part where the elevator door hits Alexander's foot. Keep reading until his mother scolds him.

Directions: Think about these questions. In the space below, write ideas or draw pictures as you think. Be ready to share your answers.

❶ What words in the text tell you why Alexander falls down?

❷ Where is Alexander's mother when he falls?

❸ According to the story, why does Alexander punch Nick?

Name _____   Date _____

Making Connections–Telling Time

Directions: Look at each clock. Write what time it tells. Draw a line to match that time of day to an event in the story.

What Time Is It?	Story Event
 (clock showing 12:00) _____	The family picks up the father from work.
 (clock showing 12:25) _____	The boys get into a fight.
 (clock showing 12:20) _____	The family is at the dentist's office.
 (clock showing 12:30) _____	The family is at the shoe store.

Making Connections-Good Dental Care

Directions: Alexander has a cavity. He needs to take better care of his teeth. In the boxes below, draw three things he can do to care for his teeth. Finish the sentence beside each box. Be sure to end each sentence with a period.

Alexander should . . .

_____

_____

_____

Alexander should . . .

_____

_____

_____

Alexander should . . .

_____

_____

_____

Name _____ Date _____

Language Learning–Contractions

Directions: A contraction is a shorter form of two words that are put together with an apostrophe in the place of the missing letter(s). Reread the after-school section. Seven different contractions are used in these pages. Write each one on a line below. Next to each one, write the two words each contraction is made of.

Language Hints!

- Put an apostrophe where the letter is missing.
- Capitalize the contraction if it starts with an *I*.

1. _____*that's*_____   _____*that*_____   _____*is*_____

2. _____   _____   _____

3. _____   _____   _____

4. _____   _____   _____

5. _____   _____   _____

6. _____   _____   _____

7. _____   _____   _____

Directions: Write a sentence that uses at least two of the contractions above.

_____

_____

Story Elements-Character

Directions: How do you think the story might be different if it were told from Anthony's point of view or Nick's point of view? Draw a cartoon showing one of the brothers' point of view.

Story Elements–Character

Directions: During the day, Alexander interacts with four different professionals: a teacher, a dentist, a salesperson, and an office worker. Which of these jobs do you think you would enjoy most? Tell why.

_____

_____

_____

_____

_____

_____

_____

_____

_____

_____

_____

Pre-Reading Picture Walk

1. Remind students that good readers make predictions before reading. A prediction is making a guess about characters or what will happen in a story. One way to do this is to examine the pictures before reading.

2. Turn to the spread where the family is eating dinner. Cover the text. Have students identify where Alexander is. Ask, "What is the family doing?" *(The family is at the table having dinner.)*

3. Look at the close-up of Alexander's face. Why do you think he looks that way? *(There is something he doesn't like for dinner.)*

4. Move to the next spread. Cover the text. Have students look at Alexander's face and predict if his mood is improving, getting worse, or staying the same.

5. Turn to the last page. It is clear that Alexander's terrible, horrible, no good, very bad day is finally over. Have students read the sentence fragment on that page and ask, "What do you think it means? *(It's a reminder that bad days happen no matter where you live.)* Why did the author end the book with this phrase? *(Writing any statement as a one-liner adds emphasis.)*

Vocabulary Overview

Key words and phrases from this section are provided below with definitions and sentences about how the words are used in the story. Introduce and discuss these important vocabulary words with students. If you think these words or other words in the story warrant more time devoted to them, there are suggestions in the introduction for other vocabulary activities (page 5).

Word	Definition	Sentence about Text
lima beans	flat, light green beans that grow on a plant	Alexander hates the taste of **lima beans.**
kissing	touching one's lips to someone else's lips as a way of showing affection	Alexander closes his eyes when there is **kissing** on a TV show.
marble	a very small toy ball made of colored glass	A **marble** is very small, so it is easy to lose.
pajamas	an outfit consisting of a top and bottom that people wear while sleeping	His railroad-train **pajamas** are the ones that Alexander hates the most.
tongue	the soft, movable part of one's mouth that is used for eating food and speaking	It hurts a lot when Alexander bites his **tongue.**

Vocabulary Activity

Directions: Choose three words from the story. Draw a picture that shows what these words mean. Label your picture.

Words from the Story

lima beans	kissing	marble	pajamas	tongue

Directions: Answer this question.

1. What food do you dislike eating at dinner?

_____

Analyzing the Literature

Provided below are discussion questions you can use in small groups, with the whole class, or for written assignments. Each question is written at two levels so you can choose the right question for each group of students. For each question, a few key points are provided for your reference as you discuss the book with students.

Story Element	Level 1	Level 2	Key Discussion Points
Setting	Where is Alexander in the evening?	Where does the evening part of the story happen? What rooms are shown?	The evening is spent at Alexander's home. We see the dining room, bathroom, and the bedroom he shares with Anthony and Nick.
Character	Who gets upset with Alexander during dinner? How do you know?	What do you think Alexander's mother is saying during dinner?	Alexander's mother gets upset with Alexander. In the illustration, she appears to be yelling at him. She may be telling him that he needs to eat his lima beans.
Plot	What bad things happen to Alexander in the tub?	How do the events in the tub add to the story?	The bathwater is too hot, Alexander gets soap in his eyes, and he loses his marble down the drain. These events bring his lousy day to a conclusion. They show that bad things just kept happening all day.
Plot	Look at the illustrations in this section. Does it seem like Alexander is still having a bad day?	Is Alexander's day improving? How do you know?	Alexander is still having a bad day; it's obvious from his facial expressions throughout this section. He looks grumpy, disgusted, upset, and frustrated.

Reader Response

Think

Alexander sees kissing on TV, and he hates it! He probably wants to change the channel.

Opinion Writing Prompt

What do you enjoy watching on TV? What do you dislike seeing on TV?

_____

_____

_____

_____

_____

_____

_____

_____

_____

Name _____ Date _____

Guided Close Reading

Closely reread the page where Alexander goes to bed.

Directions: Think about these questions. In the space below, write ideas or draw pictures as you think. Be ready to share your answers.

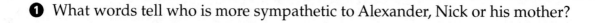

❶ What words tell who is more sympathetic to Alexander, Nick or his mother?

❷ Use the book to tell why Alexander mentions his night light.

❸ What sentence tells how the cat disappoints Alexander?

Evening

Making Connections–Life Cycle of a Lima Bean

Directions: Lima beans come from a plant. A bean plant starts as a bean, sprouts, grows into a big plant, blossoms, and then produces its own beans. In the boxes below, draw and label each stage in the life cycle of a bean plant. Cut apart your drawings and give them to a friend. Have your friend put the stages in the correct order. (Number your cards lightly on the backs so that your friend can check his or her answer.)

Name _____   Date _____

Making Connections-Cat Trouble in Australia

If Alexander does move to Australia, he may have to leave his cat behind. No cats were native to Australia. People brought cats there as pets in 1804. Some escaped. They lived in the wild. Now there are millions of feral cats. They grow to twice the size of pet cats. They kill small native Australian animals.

Directions: Read the caption for each Australian animal. Circle the ones that might be threatened by feral cats.

A quoll is about the size of a skunk. It hunts at night.

A crocodile lurks in muddy rivers.

A koala drinks no water. It gets water by eating leaves.

A kangaroo grows taller than man. It hops and keeps its baby in a pouch.

A sea turtle comes to the beach each year to lay eggs.

A numbat looks like a red striped squirrel with a pointy nose.

Language Learning–Nouns

Directions: Look at the page where the family is eating dinner. Make a list of all the nouns you can see or read on the page. Be sure to write each noun in the correct column. You should have words in each column.

Language Hints!

- A noun is a person, a place, or a thing.
- A person's name is a noun.

Person	Place	Thing

Name _____ Date _____

Story Elements-Setting

Directions: Alexander ends his day in the same place it began—in his bed. In this graphic organizer, write in order the sequence of settings (places) for Alexander's terrible, horrible, no good, very bad day.

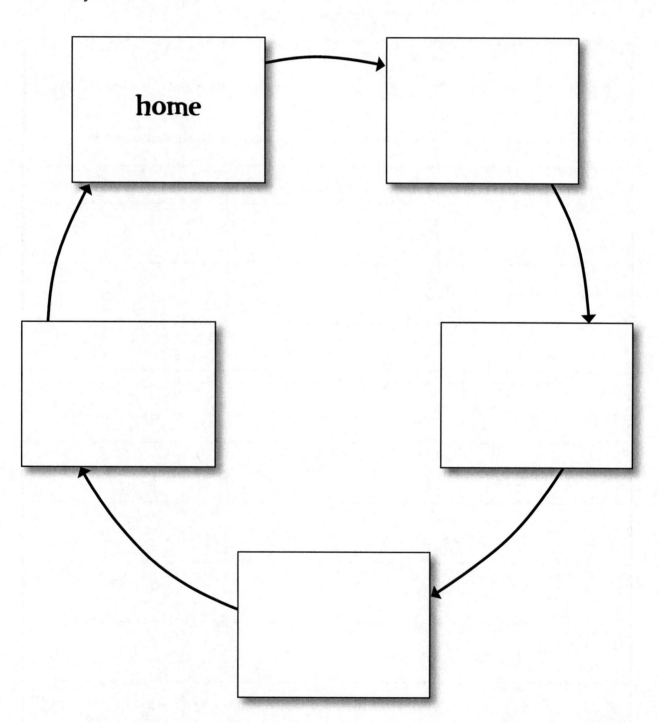

home

Story Elements–Setting

Directions: At the end of the book, there is an illustration of Alexander's bedroom. In the box below, draw a map of your bedroom as if you are looking at it from above. Label your door and window and all the furniture.

My Bedroom

Name _____ Date _____

Post-Reading Theme Thoughts

Directions: Choose a main character from *Alexander and the Terrible, Horrible, No Good, Very Bad Day*. Pretend you are that character. Draw a picture of a happy face or a sad face to show how the character would feel about each statement below. Then use words to explain your picture.

Character I Chose: _____

Statement	How Does the Character Feel? 😊 ☹	Why Does the Character Feel This Way?
You find a prize in a cereal box.		
Sometimes you have to share your friend with other friends.		
You have a cavity.		
A parent blames you when it isn't your fault.		

Culminating Activity:
Illustrate and Make a Book

Directions: Read the text on each page. Draw a picture to match. Then, cut out the pages. Put them in order and staple them together. Take your book home and read it to a family member.

Alexander Has ANOTHER Terrible, Horrible, No Good, Very Bad Day

Illustrated by _____

2

From the moment I woke up, I knew I was going to have another terrible, horrible, no good, very bad day. I knew because the cat scratched my hand. I knew because there was no hot water to wash my face. And I really knew when I sat down for breakfast.

Culminating Activity:
Illustrate and Make a Book *(cont.)*

3

There were strawberry waffles for Anthony. There were blueberry waffles for Nick. There were no chocolate chip waffles for me. I told my mother that I don't like any other flavor waffles. She didn't answer me.

4

It was raining. Anthony, Nick, and I waited on the porch. Then the bus came all of a sudden, and we had to run down the driveway. I tripped on my shoelace and landed in a mud puddle. Everyone on the bus laughed. It was a terrible, horrible, no good, very bad day.

Culminating Activity:
Illustrate and Make a Book *(cont.)*

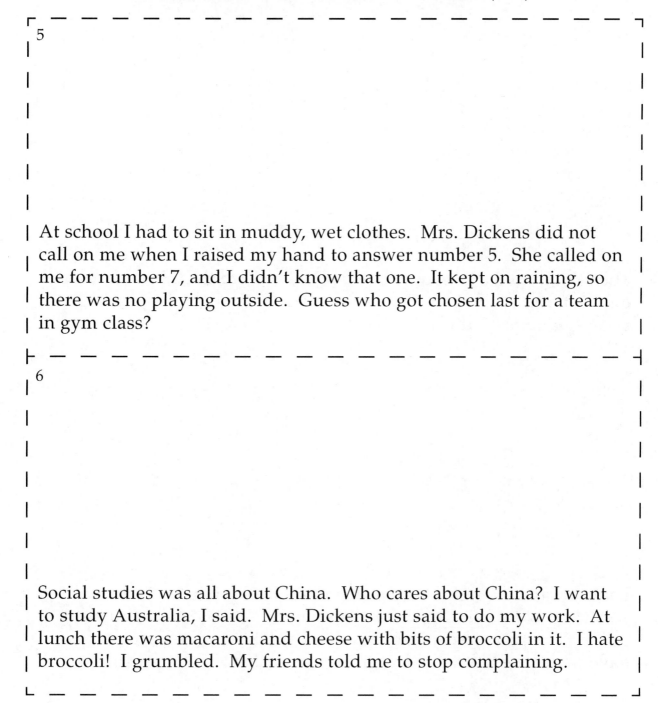

5

At school I had to sit in muddy, wet clothes. Mrs. Dickens did not call on me when I raised my hand to answer number 5. She called on me for number 7, and I didn't know that one. It kept on raining, so there was no playing outside. Guess who got chosen last for a team in gym class?

6

Social studies was all about China. Who cares about China? I want to study Australia, I said. Mrs. Dickens just said to do my work. At lunch there was macaroni and cheese with bits of broccoli in it. I hate broccoli! I grumbled. My friends told me to stop complaining.

Culminating Activity:
Illustrate and Make a Book (cont.)

7

Then Philip told a joke and Paul laughed so hard that his milk came out his nose. It sprayed all over my macaroni and cheese. I decided I wasn't hungry. (But I really was.)

8

Paul says that he's grown an inch and Philip's grown an inch and Albert's grown an inch. That makes me the shortest one. Paul said I'm the size of a preschooler. I said to Paul, I hope the next time you have a cupcake that your dog grabs it and runs away to Australia.

Culminating Activity:
Illustrate and Make a Book (cont.)

9

After school, my mom took us all to the eye doctor. Anthony's eyes were fine. Nick's eyes were fine. Dr. Lori told mom that I need glasses. I had to look at frames. I picked a pair but my mom said they cost too much. I didn't like any of the ones she pointed out. Mom chose some blue frames, but she can't make me wear them.

10

After we came home, our dog Pippa played fetch with Anthony. Then she played fetch with Nick. When I threw the ball, Pippa walked over to the corner and curled up and went to sleep. It has been a terrible, horrible, no good, very bad day.

Culminating Activity:
Illustrate and Make a Book (cont.)

11

At bedtime it was Anthony's turn to pick the story. He chose "Jack and the Beanstalk," and he knows I hate that story. Pippa wanted to sleep with Nick instead of with me, and I bit the inside of my cheek. I said I've had a terrible, horrible, no good, very bad day.

12

My mom says that tomorrow will be a better day. I hope she's right. Or else I'm moving to Australia.

Comprehension Assessment

Directions: Fill in the bubble for the best response to each question.

Morning

1. Why does Alexander say that he's going to be carsick?

(A) He wants Mrs. Gibson to stop the car.

(B) He wants Mrs. Gibson to take him back home.

(C) He hopes Mrs. Gibson will give him a seat by the window.

(D) He thinks it will make the other kids get out of the car.

At School

2. Why doesn't Mrs. Dickens like Alexander's castle picture?

(E) The drawing is sloppy.

(F) She can't see it because it's invisible.

(G) He didn't finish the drawing.

(H) Paul spills paint and ruins the drawing.

3. Explain how Alexander feels after talking to Paul.

_____

_____

_____

_____

Comprehension Assessment (cont.)

After School

4. Which sentence explains how Alexander feels about his new sneakers?

   (A) I chose blue shoes with red stripes.

   (B) They made me buy plain white shoes.

   (C) The shoe salesman said that he was all sold out.

   (D) No one can make me wear them.

Evening

5. What sentence shows how Alexander's brother added to his problems?

   (E) Nick took back the pillow he said Alexander could keep.

   (F) There was kissing on TV and Alexander hates kissing.

   (G) Alexander got soap in his eyes and lost a marble down the drain.

   (H) The cat wants to sleep with Anthony and not with Alexander.

Name _____ Date _____

Response to Literature: Analyzing the Situation

Directions: Alexander has a lot of problems during his terrible, horrible, no good, very bad day. Choose the event **you** think was the very worst. Draw the scene below. Then, answer the questions on the next page. Make sure your picture is neat and in color.

Name _____ Date _____

Response to Literature:
Analyzing the Situation (cont.)

1. When and where did this event take place?

_____

_____

_____

_____

2. Why do you think it was the worst moment of Alexander's day?

_____

_____

_____

_____

3. What happens next in the story?

_____

_____

_____

Response to Literature Rubric

Directions: Use this rubric to evaluate student responses.

Great Job	Good Work	Keep Trying
☐ You answered all three questions completely. You included many details.	☐ You answered all three questions.	☐ You did not answer all three questions.
☐ Your handwriting is very neat. There are no spelling errors.	☐ Your handwriting can be neater. There are some spelling errors.	☐ Your handwriting is not very neat. There are many spelling errors.
☐ Your picture is neat and fully colored.	☐ Your picture is neat and some of it is colored.	☐ Your picture is not very neat and/or fully colored.
☐ Creativity is clear in both the picture and the writing.	☐ Creativity is clear in either the picture or the writing.	☐ There is not much creativity in either the picture or the writing.

Teacher Comments: _____

_____

_____

_____

The responses provided here are just examples of what students may answer. Many accurate responses are possible for the questions throughout this unit.

Vocabulary Activity—Section 1:
Morning (page 16)

- Nick looks in his cereal box and finds a Junior **Undercover Agent code** ring.
- Alexander drops his **sweater** in the sink while the water is running.
- Mrs. Gibson drives four children to school in a **car pool**.
- Alexander says he is **smushed** in the back seat.
- The **terrible** day begins as soon as Alexander wakes up.

1. Getting a different seat in the car will keep him from getting **carsick**.

Guided Close Reading—Section 1:
Morning (page 19)

1. He wakes up with gum in his hair, he trips on a skateboard, and he drops his sweater in the sink with the water running.
2. (It was a going to be) a terrible, horrible, no good, very bad day.
3. The author wants the words to come out in a rush to show Alexander's frustration and emotion.

Story Elements—Section 1:
Morning (page 23)

Students will write and sequence these events (wording may differ).

1. He wakes up with gum in his hair.
2. He trips on a skateboard.
3. He drops his sweater in the sink.
4. He doesn't find a prize in his cereal box.
5. He is smushed in the back seat of the car.

Story Elements—Section 1:
Morning (page 24)

Vocabulary Activity—Section 2:
At School (page 27)

1. Alexander draws an **invisible** picture.
2. Paul's jelly roll has **coconut** sprinkles on it.
3. The **castle** picture should have shown a strong building.
4. Alexander's mom did not pack a **dessert** in his lunch.
5. Paul likes to eat **double-decker** strawberry ice cream cones.
6. Paul tells Alexander that he is only his third best friend after Philip and Albert.

Guided Close Reading—Section 2:
At School (page 30)

1. Alexander tells Paul he hopes he sits on a tack and he hopes his next ice cream cone falls apart.
2. Alexander is hurt and angry that Paul says he is not his best friend.
3. Paul tells Alexander to calm down because they are still friends. (Answers will vary.)

Making Connections—Section 2:
At School (page 31)

1. The desserts shown are cupcakes, a candy bar, and a jelly roll.
2. The healthy foods shown are milk, an apple, and a sandwich.
3. Other healthy foods that are packed in lunches include carrot sticks, celery sticks, oranges, grapes, juice, cheese and crackers, and yogurt. (Answers will vary).